THE SCIENCE OF
NUTRITION

WHY WE NEED
CARBOHYDRATES

By Molly Aloian

Crabtree Publishing Company

www.crabtreebooks.com

Crabtree Publishing Company

www.crabtreebooks.com

Author: Molly Aloian
Publishing plan research and development:
  Sean Charlebois, Reagan Miller
Editors: Sarah Eason, Nick Hunter, Lynn Peppas
Proofreaders: Robyn Hardyman, Kathy Middleton
Project coordinator: Kathy Middleton
Design: Calcium
Photo Research: Susannah Jayes
Print coordinator: Katherine Berti
Production coordinator and prepress technician:
  Ken Wright
Series consultant: Julie Negrin

Picture credits:
Fotolia: Zentilia 35
Istockphoto: Aldomurillo 27, Onebluelight 25
Photolibrary: Carol and Mike Werner 18
Rex Features: Giuliano Bevilacqua 30
Shutterstock: cover, Hintau Aliaksei 16, Apollofoto 4,
  Diego Cervo 24, Mikael Damkier 8, Elena Elisseeva 9,
  14, 23, Fancy 17, David Gilder 6, Mandy Godbehear 43,
  Icyimage 19, Italianestro 13, Ivaylo Ivanov 10, Jeabjeab 7,
  Evgeny Karandaev 38l, LensKiss 42, Leungchopan 39,
  Jason Maehl 28, Mirrormere 38r, Monkey Business
  Images 26, 34, 37, 41, Netfalls 31, Thomas M Perkins 15,
  Alexander Raths 21, Reika 38c, Elena Schweitzer 11, Jason
  Stitt 22, Suzanne Tucker 12, Vicente Barcelo Varona 20,
  Wavebreakmedia ltd 29, 32, ZCW 40

Library and Archives Canada Cataloguing in Publication

Aloian, Molly
    Why we need carbohydrates / Molly Aloian.

(The science of nutrition)
Includes index.
Issued also in electronic format.
ISBN 978-0-7787-1686-0 (bound).--ISBN 978-0-7787-1693-8 (pbk.)

      1. Carbohydrates in the body--Juvenile literature.
I. Title. II. Series: Science of nutrition (St. Catharines, Ont.)

QP701.A46 2011   j612'.01578   C2011-900203-5

Library of Congress Cataloging-in-Publication Data

Aloian, Molly.
  Why we need carbohydrates / Molly Aloian.
      p. cm. -- (The science of nutrition)
  Includes index.
  ISBN 978-0-7787-1693-8 (pbk. : alk. paper) -- ISBN 978-0-7787-1686-0
(reinforced library binding : alk. paper) -- ISBN 978-1-4271-9677-4
(electronic (pdf))
  1. Carbohydrates in human nutrition--Juvenile literature. I. Title.
II. Series.

  QP701.A46 2011
  612'.01578--dc22

                                        2010052739

Crabtree Publishing Company

Printed in the U.S.A./022011/CJ20101228

www.crabtreebooks.com   1-800-387-7650

Published in Canada
Crabtree Publishing
616 Welland Ave.
St. Catharines, Ontario
L2M 5V6

Published in the United States
Crabtree Publishing
PMB 59051
350 Fifth Avenue, 59th Floor
New York, New York 10118

Published in the United Kingdom
Crabtree Publishing
Maritime House
Basin Road North, Hove
BN41 1WR

Published in Australia
Crabtree Publishing
386 Mt. Alexander Rd.
Ascot Vale (Melbourne)
VIC 3032

CONTENTS

FOOD FOR FUEL

When you eat food, for example, a cheese and tomato sandwich, you might think you are just eating bread, cheese, and tomatoes. But you are eating much more than that. Locked away inside food are important nutrients that you need, not just to stay healthy, but also to stay alive.

Energy in food

Your body needs energy all the time—even when you are asleep! **Nutrients** called carbohydrates, protein, and fats give you the energy you need. In a cheese sandwich, the bread is rich in carbohydrates, and the cheese contains fats and protein. Most of the energy you need should come from carbohydrates and protein. Your body needs fat, but not too much. Too much fat is not healthy for your heart and **arteries**.

Noodles are rich in carbohydrates, the nutrient that gives you the energy you need every day.

The food pyramid shows healthy foods only. It does not include foods such as cookies and chips, which are high in salt, fat, or sugar.

Grains
Grains give you energy, but they also contain some protein and other nutrients.

Vegetables and fruits
You should eat a wide range from these two groups to get all the nutrients you need.

Oils and fats
These foods should not be overeaten.

Milk
This group of foods is rich in protein but can also be high in fat.

Meat and beans
These foods are rich in protein, although meats can also be high in fat.

You need nutrients

You need a balance of carbohydrates, protein, and fat in your food to stay healthy. You also need tiny amounts of nutrients called vitamins and minerals. Luckily, each nutrient is found in many different foods, so you can choose healthy food that you like.

The food pyramid divides healthy food into six different groups. Choosing food from these groups will give you all the nutrients you need.

This book is about carbohydrates. This nutrient gives you most of the energy you need to lead a healthy lifestyle.

WHAT ARE CARBOHYDRATES?

Your body needs energy every day. The energy in food fuels your body like the gasoline in a car engine. Food gives you the energy to get up and ride your bike to school. Energy fuels your brain so you can read a book and solve difficult math problems. But where does all that energy come from? The answer is easy—carbohydrates!

Body Talk

Most of the carbohydrates in food come from plants such as cereals, potatoes, and rice. Your body can break down carbohydrates quickly to release energy to fuel the body. It can also store carbohydrates as fat and use them for energy later.

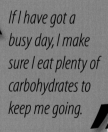

If I have got a busy day, I make sure I eat plenty of carbohydrates to keep me going.

Food gives you the energy you need to keep fit.

Cannot live without it…

Carbohydrates are one of the main nutrients that people need to survive. Sugars, starches, and most kinds of fiber are all carbohydrates. Sugars are sweet, and they give many foods their yummy tastes. Foods such as fruits and honey are rich in natural sugars.

Starches are not as sweet, but they help make a balanced meal. Foods such as breakfast cereals, potatoes, and pasta contain starch. The body breaks down the starch to release the energy in the food.

Workers plant rice in a paddy field in Southeast Asia. Rice is an important source of carbohydrates for many people around the world.

Did you know?

There are many different kinds of carbohydrates, but they are all made up of carbon, hydrogen, and oxygen. These elements are the building blocks of everything in the universe. Elements are substances that are made up of just one kind of **atom**. A simple sugar is made up of groups of carbon, hydrogen, and oxygen. They are arranged in a ring. The rings can be linked together, just like rings of paper can be linked to make a paper chain.

Simple or complicated

Sugars are the simplest kind of carbohydrate. Two examples of simple sugars are glucose and fructose. You have glucose in your blood—it is your body's most important source of energy. Fructose is found in fruits. Both glucose and fructose contain six carbon atoms in each **molecule**.

One or two?

Simple sugars such as glucose and fructose are called monosaccharides. *Mono* is the Latin word for "one," and *saccharide* comes from the Latin word meaning "sugar." Simple sugars are good sources of immediate energy.

A disaccharide is two simple sugars joined together. (*Di* means "two.") Lactose, the sugar found in milk, is an example of a disaccharide.

Complex carbohydrates

A polysaccharide is made up of more than two saccharides joined together. (*Poly* means "many.") Polysaccharides are also called complex carbohydrates. The starch found in cereals and vegetables is a complex carbohydrate. Starch is made up of thousands of glucose molecules joined together.

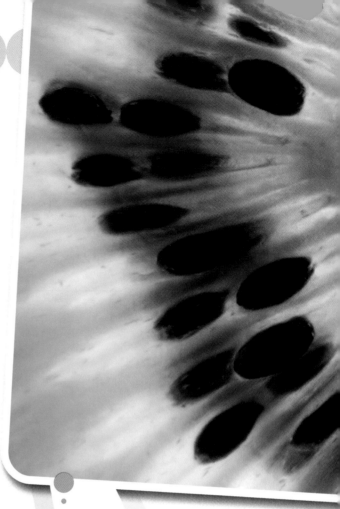

Kiwi fruits are rich in fructose—a simple sugar that gives the body instant energy.

Body Talk

Some people are lactose intolerant. This means they have trouble digesting a type of sugar called lactose.

Did you know?

The carbon, hydrogen, and oxygen in all simple sugars are found in a 1:2:1 ratio—one part carbon, two parts hydrogen, and one part oxygen.

Sweetcorn contains starch and fiber. These carbohydrates are good sources of slow-release energy, making you feel fuller for longer.

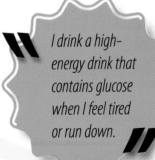

I drink a high-energy drink that contains glucose when I feel tired or run down.

Bulking up on fiber

Fiber is a complex carbohydrate we get when we eat plants. There are different types of fiber, and each type does a different job in your body. Foods that are rich in fiber add bulk to your meals. This makes you feel full faster and keeps you feeling full for a longer period of time.

WE'RE RICH—IN CARBOHYDRATES!

Many foods contain the carbohydrates people need for energy. Keep reading to find out how many of these foods you eat on a daily basis and how you can add more healthy carbohydrates to give you a balanced diet. You might be surprised to find out where all of your energy is coming from!

Carbohydrates such as potatoes release energy slowly and fuel your body for longer.

Pass the pasta!

There are hundreds of foods that are rich in carbohydrates. Pasta is a popular food that is rich in carbohydrates. It fuels your brain and muscles and provides energy. People often eat pasta with other foods, such as beans, cheese, fish, meat, olive oil, tomato sauce, and vegetables. By eating pasta with these other foods, the pasta is both nutritious and satisfying.

Did you know?

Most food experts say that between 45 percent to 65 percent of your total daily **calories** should come from carbohydrates.

Body Talk

Hunger is your body's physical need for food. A cone-shaped part of your brain, called the hypothalamus, tells you that you are hungry when your body needs food. It also tells you that you are feeling thirsty when your body needs water.

Other carbs

Breakfast cereals, bread, fruits, pasta, potatoes, and vegetables are other foods that contain carbohydrates. These foods contain complex carbohydrates. Cake, cookies, and candy also contain carbohydrates, but they contain simple sugars. These carbohydrates are not as good for you because your body digests them quickly and receives only a short burst of energy in return. Simple sugars are often **processed** or **refined**, which makes them taste better but removes important nutrients, including certain vitamins and minerals such as iron.

When I feel hungry, I snack on healthy foods such as fruit and raw vegetables instead of sweets.

Sugary foods such as cookies give you a quick burst of energy. But eating too much sugar is bad for your teeth, so keep this type of food for a treat.

11

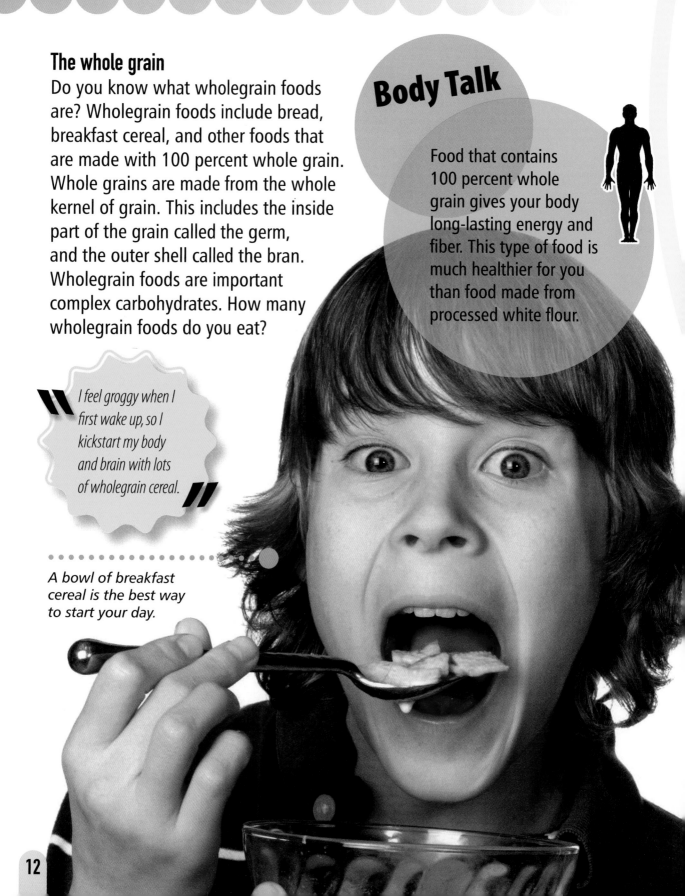

The whole grain

Do you know what wholegrain foods are? Wholegrain foods include bread, breakfast cereal, and other foods that are made with 100 percent whole grain. Whole grains are made from the whole kernel of grain. This includes the inside part of the grain called the germ, and the outer shell called the bran. Wholegrain foods are important complex carbohydrates. How many wholegrain foods do you eat?

Body Talk

Food that contains 100 percent whole grain gives your body long-lasting energy and fiber. This type of food is much healthier for you than food made from processed white flour.

I feel groggy when I first wake up, so I kickstart my body and brain with lots of wholegrain cereal.

A bowl of breakfast cereal is the best way to start your day.

Three whole servings

Wholegrain foods include brown rice, wild rice, bulgur wheat, and quinoa. Buckwheat flour, corn flour, spelt flour, and oat flour are made using whole grain foods. The **United States Department of Agriculture (USDA)** suggests that people eat at least three servings of whole grains every day. Many food manufacturers are using more whole grains in breakfast cereals, bread, and pasta. They are using forms of wholegrain flour to make breads that are very similar to white bread in texture and taste.

These ears of wheat contain the cereal grain used to make carbohydrate-rich foods such as bread and pasta.

Did you know?

Not only is quinoa an energy-packed carbohydrate, it is also an excellent source of protein. The grain originally comes from the Andes in South America, where it has been grown for thousands of years. Nutritionists call quinoa a "supergrain" because it is packed with valuable nutrients.

Running on empty

The phrase empty calories describes foods that are high in energy but low in vital nutrients such as vitamins, minerals, and fiber. Your body needs energy for fuel, but it also needs essential nutrients to stay healthy. Foods with empty calories include hard candy, chocolate bars, ice cream, and soda pop.

Smooth and sweet

Most people enjoy eating sugary foods. The simple sugars in these foods give them smooth textures and sweet tastes. Simple sugars make cookies and candy crispy. They make ice cream and fudge creamy.

Sugary foods give you the energy your body needs to work, but too much sugar is unhealthy. Your body stores unused sugar as fat, and sugary foods are bad for your teeth.

Ice cream is a delicious treat, but it is full of sugar and lacks vital nutrients such as vitamins and minerals.

I get an instant energy high when I eat candy, but I always feel really tired later on.

Brightly colored candy is full of empty calories.

What you need:

1. 1 package of dry active yeast
2. 1 cup (240 ml) of very warm water
3. 2 tablespoons (30 ml) of sugar
4. 1 large balloon
5. 1 empty 16 fluid ounce (500 ml) bottle

Instructions:

1. Stretch out the balloon a little, then set it aside.
2. Add the yeast and the sugar to the cup of warm water and stir well.
3. Once the yeast and sugar have dissolved, pour the mixture into the bottle. Notice how the water bubbles as the yeast produces carbon dioxide gas.
4. Attach the balloon to the mouth of the bottle and set it aside. After several minutes you will see that the balloon has inflated.

What just happened:

As the yeast feeds on the sugar, it produces carbon dioxide. The carbon dioxide slowly fills the balloon. A similar process happens as bread rises. Carbon dioxide from yeast fills thousands of balloon-like bubbles in the dough. Once the bread has baked, this is what gives the loaf its airy texture.

FABULOUS FIBER

Although neither type nourishes the body, both soluble and insoluble fiber promote good health in many ways. Eating plenty of fiber can help reduce your risk of developing many health problems, including constipation, **diabetes**, and heart disease.

Fiber is an important complex carbohydrate, but your body cannot digest it. Fiber is found in all plants that we eat as food. For example, fruits, vegetables, grains, and legumes are rich in fiber.

Fiber fills you up

Fiber is tough, so your body cannot break it down into sugar molecules. As a result, the fiber passes through the body undigested. The fiber in food does not supply you with any calories, but it is still good to eat. It makes you feel full and helps your body digest your food. There are different kinds of fiber and eating a wide variety of foods allows you to get all you need.

Flax seed is one of the richest sources of fiber.

Soluble fiber

Soluble fiber partially dissolves in water. **Pectin** and gums are soluble fibers. Apples and citrus fruits have a lot of pectin. An average-size apple with the peel contains about 0.1 ounces (3.6 g) of fiber.

Insoluble fiber

Insoluble fiber does not dissolve in water. Cellulose and hemicellulose are insoluble fibers. They are found in the cell walls of plants, in the protective outer layer of whole grains, and in the skins of fruits and vegetables. The next time you eat a baked potato, make sure you eat the skin to get the fiber your body needs.

Did you know?

The sugars in plant fibers are joined together with strong bonds. Your body's digestive system cannot break the bonds that hold these carbohydrates together. The more fiber a food has, the less digestible are its carbohydrates, and so the less sugar it can deliver to your body.

Apples are a healthy snack–full of the natural sugars and fiber your body needs to stay healthy.

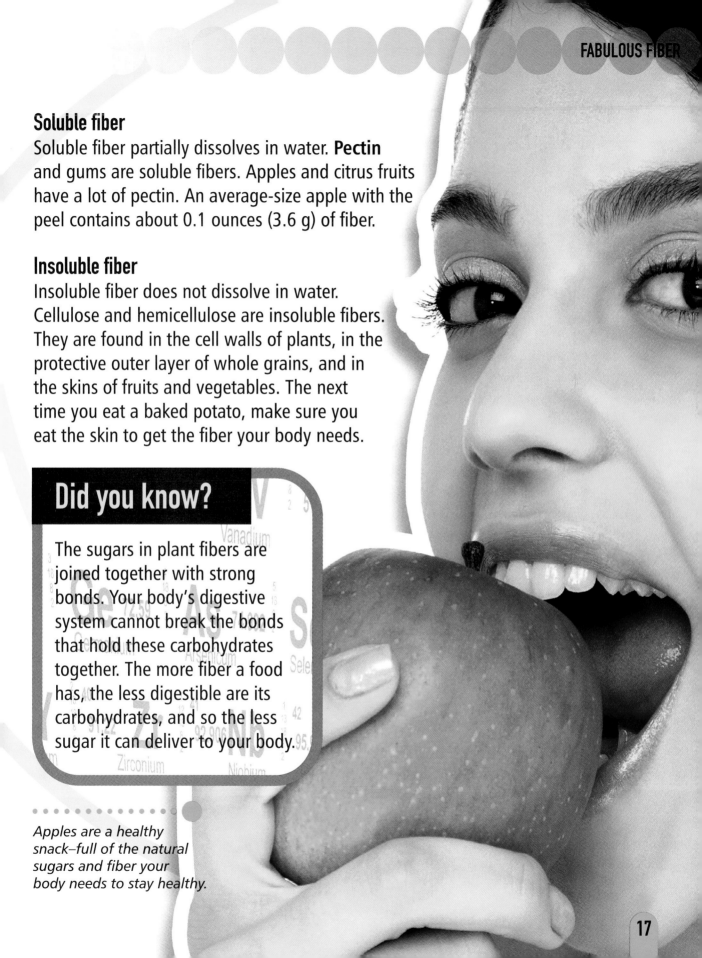

HOW MUCH IS ENOUGH?

It is important to have enough glucose in your bloodstream, so that your body's cells have a constant supply of energy. But too much glucose in your blood can be dangerous, and a diet too high in carbohydrates can cause health problems.

Healthy levels

Keeping your body's blood sugar level within a healthy range is a delicate balance. After you eat a meal, extra glucose enters the bloodstream. The liver then removes some of the glucose and stores it as glycogen. If you do not eat for a while and the body has used up all the glucose in the bloodstream, your liver breaks down this stored glycogen into glucose. The liver then releases the glucose into the blood, so the body's cells can get the energy they need.

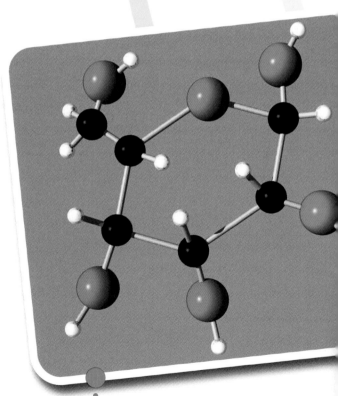

A glucose molecule is made up of six carbon atoms (black), six oxygen atoms (red), and 12 hydrogen atoms (white).

Helpful hormones

Body chemicals called **hormones** help regulate the glucose levels in your body. Insulin is a hormone that works to lower your blood sugar level. Like insulin, glucagon is produced in the pancreas. It helps raise your blood sugar level if it falls too low.

Epinephrine is another hormone that helps provide you with extra bursts of energy. It is called the "fight or flight" hormone. Both insulin and glucagon ensure that all the cells in your body, especially your brain cells, have a steady supply of blood sugar.

If I do not eat enough carbs, I feel really tired.

It is hard to concentrate when you do not eat enough carbohydrates because your body is not getting the energy it needs.

More than enough

If there is too much glucose in your bloodstream, and all of the glycogen storage sites are filled, the extra glucose is changed into fat and you gain weight. Being overweight is bad for your health. It causes problems such as high blood pressure and heart disease. Some people also develop a condition called diabetes.

High blood sugar

People with type 1 diabetes cannot make enough insulin, so their cells cannot absorb sugar. People with type 2 diabetes have a different kind of problem—the body does not respond well to insulin,

Body Talk

The pancreas releases a hormone called insulin into the blood when there is too much glucose in the body. Glucagon is released when there is too little glucose.

and the body does not absorb enough sugar. This condition, called insulin resistance, causes blood sugar and insulin levels to stay high a long time after eating. Over time, insulin-making cells wear out. The body's insulin production slows down and eventually stops.

A diabetic uses a machine to test the level of sugar in her blood.

Cutting back

Research has shown that a lack of exercise and being overweight can lead to insulin resistance. Eating a lot of processed carbohydrates can also contribute to the problem. Cutting back on refined grains and eating more whole grains can help prevent and improve insulin resistance. Eating whole grains can also help prevent type 2 diabetes, heart disease, certain cancers, and other health problems.

Did you know?

Researchers estimate that 90 percent of type 2 diabetes cases could be prevented through a combination of a healthy diet and an active lifestyle.

An insulin injection is needed if a diabetic's blood sugar levels are too high. The insulin mops up the extra sugar in the bloodstream.

My doctor said I was eating too many carbohydrates, which was upsetting my blood sugar level. It left me feeling really irritable and tired.

Carbohydrates for life

Life would not exist without carbohydrates—they provide people with energy. Your body needs different carbs to remain strong and healthy. Simple carbohydrates are sweet and make food taste good, but complex carbs are much better for your body. They make you feel fuller for longer, and they contain other nutrients such as vitamins and minerals.

Costs less, lasts longer

Carb-rich foods are often less expensive than foods that are rich in protein and fat, such as meat. They are also easier to store because they do not spoil as quickly.

I always buy a lot of healthy carbohydrates when I shop. They taste great, last a long time, and cost a lot less than many other foods.

Carbs are great for energy, but, like all food, best if eaten in moderation!

Edamame beans are a healthy source of carbs, protein, and micronutrients.

Low-carb diets

Some people who are trying to lose weight eat a low-carb diet, with very few carbohydrates. They think that carbohydrates are bad for you and make you gain weight. In the 1970s, Dr. Robert Atkins created a low-carb, high-fat, high-protein diet called the Atkins diet. This diet became popular with people who wanted to lose weight.

The whole story

Some people believe that low-carb diets may help them lose weight faster than low-fat diets. But the long term health risks have not been fully proven. It is always best to eat a balanced diet of complex carbohydrates, lean proteins, and healthy fats. You should be suspicious of any diet that tells you that one of these macronutrients is "bad" for you.

Body Talk

Carbohydrates, fats, proteins, and water are called macronutrients because your body needs these nutrients in large amounts. (The word *macro* means "large.") Vitamins and minerals are micronutrients because your body needs them in smaller amounts. (The word *micro* means "small.")

IT'S ON THE LABEL

G overnments in both the United States and Canada require packaged foods to have nutrition labels so that people know what they are eating. Reading food labels is a good way to learn more about the different ingredients in food.

Start reading

Food labels must contain a basic list of ingredients. They should also show specific information about serving size, total calories, calories from fat, and other important information. When you are reading a food label, bear in mind that your body needs some fat, salt, and sugar. Try not to eat too much fat, salt, and sugar. They might make foods taste better, but they do not make them healthier.

It is important to check the labels on food to make sure you know what you are eating.

A balanced diet

Food labels try to show how one serving of the packaged food fits into a daily balanced diet. For example, for a 2,000-calorie per day diet, some health experts suggest that about 600 calories (2.3 ounces or 65 g) should be from fat.

Did you know?

Food labels must contain the Percent Daily Value. This is the percentage of the suggested daily amount of a nutrient in a food serving based on a 2,000-calorie diet. Over the course of one day, the Percent Daily Values of each nutrient in the different foods you eat should add up to about 100 percent.

Try this...

Look at a food label. Can you see that all the different types of sugars have the letters "-ose" at the end of their names? Glucose, fructose, mannose, and xylose are all different types of sugars. When you see ingredients with "-ose" at the end on a food label, it means they are sugars.

The food label on this bag of potatoes tells you that they are rich in carbohydrates. The label shows how much of each nutrient is in one potato and in a 3.5 ounce (100 g) serving.

Cook on full power

Turn			
Cook on full power	4 mins	3½ mins	3 mins
Stand	2 mins	2 mins	2 mins
Total time	10 mins	9 mins	8 mins

Adjust times according to your particular oven. (For fan-assisted ovens cooking times should be reduced. For best results, refer to the manufacturer's handbook).

All appliances vary, these are guidelines only.

Check food is piping hot before serving.

Why not use half the recommended microwave time to soften the potato before baking? Then bake the potato for half of the recommended oven period for an authentic, oven-crispy potato in almost half the time!

Nutrition

Typical composition	1 potato (approx 175g) provides	100g provides
Energy	586kJ	335kJ
	138kcal	79kcal
Protein	3.7g	2.1g
Carbohydrate	30.1g	17.2g
of which sugars	1.1g	0.6g
Fat	0.4g	0.2g
of which saturates	trace	trace
Fibre	2.3g	1.3g
Sodium	trace	trace
Vitamins/Minerals		
Thiamin (Vitamin B1)	0.37mg (26% RDA)	0.21mg (15% RDA)
Folic Acid	61µg (31% RDA)	35µg (18% RDA)

RDA = Recommended Daily Allowance.

> *I use food labels to compare foods. They tell you everything you need to know, from which food has more fiber and which food has more fat, to which has more calories per serving.*

Greatest to least

The ingredients on a food label are listed in order from the greatest to the least percentage by weight. For example, the first ingredient on a box of crackers might be flour. This means that flour makes up most of the cracker's weight.

More or less

When you are reading food labels, bear in mind that different people need different amounts of nutrients. For example, a young person might need more or less than the average 2,000 calories per day. Factors that determine how many calories you need include your age, whether you are male or female, and how active you are on a daily basis. For the same reasons, young people may need more or less of certain nutrients, such as calcium, protein, and iron.

Every member of a family needs different amounts of nutrients to stay healthy. Children need more fat as a percentage of their diet because their bodies are still growing.

Did you know?

Most nutrients are measured in grams, also written as g. There are 28 grams in one ounce. Some nutrients are measured in smaller units called milligrams, or mg. Milligrams are very tiny—there are 1,000 milligrams in one gram.

How many nutrients you get from your food depends on the serving size. The food label gives information based on a typical serving, usually 3.5 ounces (100 g).

Serving size

The nutrition label always lists a serving size, which is an amount of food, such as one cup (240 ml) of cereal, two cookies, or five pretzels. The nutrition label tells you how many nutrients are in the serving. Serving sizes also help people understand and keep track of how much food they are eating.

Do your math!

The nutrition label should also tell you how many servings are contained in that package of food. If there are 15 servings in a box of cookies and each serving is two cookies, you have enough for all 30 kids in your class to have one cookie each. Math comes in handy with food labels.

FUEL FOR THE BODY

Carbohydrates are very important nutrients. They provide your body with the energy it needs for physical activities and help keep your brain and other organs working properly. Your body could not function without carbohydrates.

Muscles need carbs

No matter what sports you play or what activities you do, carbohydrates are the most important source of energy in food. Carbohydrates provide the energy that your muscles need to work properly. Your digestive system breaks down the carbs into smaller glucose molecules. Your muscles then use glucose as fuel to move around. Your liver and your muscles store extra sugar as glycogen. Any extra glucose is stored as fat–that is why it is important not to overeat.

You will need a lot of carbs to give you enough energy for sports and activities such as climbing.

Body Talk

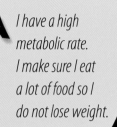

The term basal metabolism describes the amount of energy your body uses while resting, to carry out basic functions such as breathing and making your heart pump blood around the body. A person with a high basal metabolism needs more energy than a person with a low basal metabolism. People with high metabolisms need more calories to provide them with enough energy.

I have a high metabolic rate. I make sure I eat a lot of food so I do not lose weight.

It is not just physical exercise that uses up energy–your brain needs fuel, too!

Exercise and energy

Glycogen is the source of energy most often used for exercise. Your body needs it for short, intense bursts of exercise, such as sprinting or weight lifting, because your body can release the glycogen very quickly. Glycogen supplies energy during the first few minutes of any sport. During long, slow periods of exercise, your body starts to burn fat for energy, but glycogen is still needed to help break the fat down so the muscles can use the energy it contains.

Carbohydrate calories

Eating carbohydrates helps prevent your body from using protein as a source of energy. If your body does not have enough carbs, it breaks down protein to make the glucose to fuel your body. Protein provides the building blocks for muscles, bones, skin, hair, and other tissues, so relying on protein for energy can ultimately limit your body's ability to build and maintain tissues.

Gold-medal Olympic champion Michael Phelps eats a carefully balanced diet to make sure his body stays in peak condition.

Body Talk

Carbohydrates stored as glycogen is an easily accessible source of energy for exercise. But how long does this energy supply last? It depends on the length and intensity of the exercise and can range anywhere from 30 to 90 minutes or more. Carbohydrates are like the gasoline in a car. Just like a car needs fuel to move, your body needs glucose to move.

> I tried a really low-carb diet, but I could not think straight at school, and I just wanted to sleep all the time.

When you are asleep, your body uses energy to carry out basic body functions such as breathing and keeping your heart beating.

Did you know?

Even when you are asleep, neurons in your brain use the energy from food to repair and rebuild themselves.

Brain power

Energy is not just for movement. Your brain uses energy when you think. Your brain needs a constant supply of glucose to work properly, and it gets used up quickly during mental activity. In fact, your brain cells need twice as much energy than any other cell in your body, including the cells that make up your muscles. If you are not eating enough carb-rich food, you are cutting off your brain's main energy supply. This will make you feel tired and you will not feel like doing anything.

DIGESTING CARBOHYDRATES

When I am really hungry, my stomach starts making growling noises. It can get very loud, and it is a bit embarrassing.

In order for your body to use carbohydrates, they must be broken down into their simplest form. It takes different amounts of time for the body to break down simple sugars and complex carbs into a form your body can use. This is the job of your digestive system.

Body Talk

Saliva kills bacteria and softens and moistens the starch in the food that you eat. You release more than two pints (1 l) of saliva into your mouth every day!

Seeing and smelling

The process of digesting carbohydrates can actually begin before you have any food in your mouth! When you see or smell a fresh-baked cookie or a slice of warm pizza and your mouth starts watering, the digestion process has begun. The "water" in your mouth is called saliva—and it is the first part of the digestive process.

Eating a pizza will get your digestive juices flowing.

It all starts in the mouth

The saliva in your mouth contains an important digestive **enzyme**, called amylase. Chewing food grinds the food up and mixes it with saliva. The amylase then starts to break down starches into sugars. When you swallow, the food mush travels down the **esophagus** and into the stomach.

Once the carbs come into contact with the acids in your stomach, the amylase stops working. The acids then get to work on your food, and the walls of the stomach churn the partially digested liquid, called **chyme**, to break it down further.

Into the pancreas and small intestine

The chyme passes from your stomach into the small **intestine**. This is where the real process of digestion takes place. The small intestine and an organ called the pancreas produce digestive enzymes. Amylase in the pancreas breaks starch into disaccharides and polysaccharides. Enzymes from the cells of the small-intestinal wall break any remaining disaccharides into monosaccharides. Fiber is not digested by the small intestine. It travels into the **colon**.

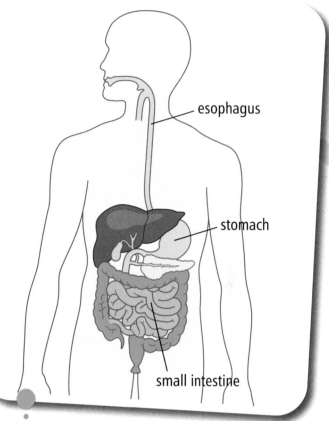

esophagus

stomach

small intestine

Food passes down the esophagus into the stomach. The partially digested food then moves to the small intestine.

Did you know?

An apple a day really does keep the doctor away! Apples are high in fiber and contain important **antioxidants**. These can help to neutralize substances that can cause health problems such as heart disease and cancer.

Body Talk

You have a small intestine and a large intestine. The large intestine is between the small intestine and the **rectum**. It is about twice as large in diameter as the small intestine. The large intestine is U-shaped and is usually between five and six feet (1.5 and 1.8 m) long. The small intestine is about 22 feet (7 m) long.

Mechanical and chemical

Digestion is both mechanical and chemical. Mechanical digestion is your body physically breaking up food into smaller pieces. You do this using your teeth and saliva and by churning food in your stomach. Mechanical digestion also involves the process known as **peristalsis**. Peristalsis is carried out by smooth muscle within the body and is responsible for the movement of food through the digestive tract. Chemical digestion is your body breaking apart long chains of food molecules into smaller molecules using digestive enzymes.

The process of mechanical digestion begins as soon as you put food in your mouth.

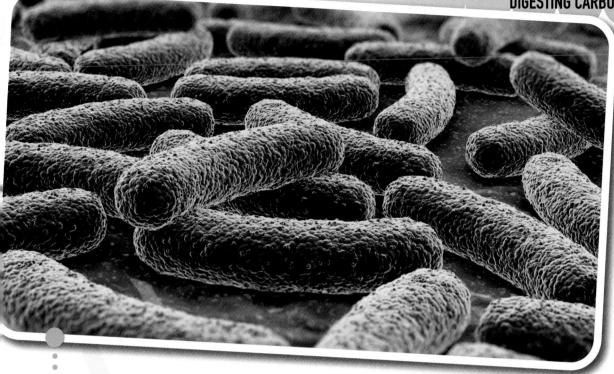

Friendly bacteria live on the walls of your intestines.
These microscopic organisms do an important job. They help
your body break down and release the nutrients in food.

Did you know?

The amount of time your body needs to process food through mechanical and chemical digestion varies from person to person. In healthy adults, it can take anywhere between 24 hours and 72 hours. After you eat, food typically remains in your stomach and small intestine for six to eight hours. The large intestine is capable of holding undigested food waste for several days!

Everyday enzymes

Your body uses digestive enzymes to speed up the process of chemical digestion. Complex molecules, including carbohydrates, are broken down into smaller molecules. These smaller molecules can then be absorbed by your cells.

There are eight known digestive enzymes that are responsible for chemical digestion. These enzymes are: nuclease, protease, collagenase, lipase, amylase, elastase, trypsin, and chymotrypsin.

CELL BOOSTERS

Simple sugars such as glucose, fructose, and galactose, are absorbed into cells in the intestine. After the sugars are absorbed, they are transported to the liver, where galactose and fructose are converted to glucose and released into the bloodstream.

Any organs that need energy take up glucose from the blood. Some of the glucose in the blood is also stored in the liver or muscles as glycogen. This process is called glycogenesis. Glucose can also be converted to fat and stored in the body.

Releasing energy

The glucose in your blood supplies all the cells and tissues of your body with glucose. But how does your body get energy out of glucose? It gets energy through a process called **respiration**.

Glucose molecules (yellow) travel around the body in the bloodstream. The body's cells and tissues also need oxygen to get the energy from food.

Body Talk

Glycogen is the form of carbohydrate that animals store. It is made up of long chains of glucose molecules. Your body converts glucose to glycogen in the liver and muscle cells. Glycogen in the liver is readily available for energy and also to maintain the levels of sugar in the blood. Muscle glycogen is stored for when you need to use muscles.

Respiration is a chemical reaction that takes place inside your body's cells. It needs glucose and oxygen, which you get when you breathe in from the air. When you breathe, oxygen in the air passes into your lungs. Oxygen then passes through tiny blood vessels, called capillaries, deep inside your lungs. Red blood cells take the oxygen to all the body's cells and tissues. There it reacts with glucose, forming carbon dioxide and water. Energy is released in the process.

Breathing supplies the body with the oxygen it needs to release the energy in food.

GLYCEMIC INDEX

Grouping carbohydrates into simple sugars and complex carbs makes sense on a chemical level. But you might still be wondering what happens to all the different kinds of carbs inside your body. Not all carbs have the same effect. For example, the starch found in potatoes and brown bread is a complex carbohydrate. However, your body can convert this starch to blood sugar almost as quickly as it processes pure glucose.

The fructose in fruit is a simple carbohydrate like glucose, but it has little effect on your blood sugar level.

Measuring the effects of carbs

A new system, called the glycemic index (GI), measures the effects of different carbohydrates on the body's blood sugar level. It compares different carbohydrates based on how quickly and how much they boost blood sugar compared to pure glucose. Foods with a high glycemic index are digested quickly and cause a quick spike in blood sugar just like glucose. The body digests food with a low glycemic index much more slowly. This causes a lower, gentler change in blood sugar levels.

High GI   *Medium GI*   *Low GI*

Different foods have different glycemic index value.

High and low

The glycemic index uses glucose as the standard and gives it a value of 100. Foods with a score of 70 or higher are said to have a high glycemic index. These include foods such as baked potatoes, white rice, and breakfast cereals such as cornflakes.

Foods with a score of 55 or below have a low glycemic index. These include most fruits and vegetables, meat, dairy products, nuts, and wholegrain food products.

Did you know?

Grains that have been milled and refined, which removes the bran and germ, have a higher glycemic index than whole grains. That is because your body finds it easier to digest refined food.

When you have a cold, you cannot smell your food or really taste it.

Body Talk

Have you ever noticed that your food is not very tasty when you have a stuffy nose from a cold? This is because a lot of what you think you taste you actually smell. Chocolate ice cream tastes sweet because it contains a lot of sugar, but it also tastes like chocolate. The chocolate flavor is due to your sense of smell, not taste.

FOOD ALLERGIES AND SPECIAL DIETS

Some people cannot eat certain foods. Their bodies react to substances in the food in what is known as a food allergy. Food allergies are caused by the body's immune system. The immune system reacts to specific proteins in the food as if they were harmful substances. Research has shown that between five and six percent of young children and three to four percent of adults in North America are affected by food allergies. As people eat more unusual foods, the problems may get worse.

Mistaken identity

The **immune system** of a person with a food allergy mistakes the proteins in some foods as harmful substances. The first time the person eats the food, the immune system responds by creating **antibodies** against the protein. When the person eats the food again, his or her body releases the antibodies, along with a chemical named **histamine**, to fight off the protein.

Foods that commonly cause allergic reactions include shellfish such as clams.

Reacting badly

Histamine causes an immediate reaction, usually seen as a runny nose and watery eyes. It can also cause skin rashes and can shrink the airways, making it difficult to breathe. In the most extreme cases, food allergies can be **fatal**. Any food can cause an allergic reaction, but a few foods seem to be responsible for most food allergies.

> I am allergic to peanuts. Even being close to someone eating peanuts causes my body to react. It is really scary.

Did you know?

One of the most common food allergies involves nuts. Someone who has a nut allergy will usually have it for the rest of their life. Almonds, Brazil nuts, cashew nuts, hazelnuts, and walnuts are most likely to cause an allergic reaction, and sometimes this can be fatal. Every year, hundreds of people in North America die from allergic reactions to nuts. Because nut allergies can be so dangerous, food labels must clearly show if foods contain nuts—even trace amounts can be fatal.

Peanut butter sandwiches taste great, but peanuts are one of the most common causes of food allergies. They can cause a severe allergic reaction. Many people die each year from peanut allergies.

Drinking milk may seem natural to most people, but people with a lactose intolerance cannot digest lactose–the natural sugar found in milk.

What is a food intolerance?

A food intolerance is a sensitivity to some type of food or ingredient. A food intolerance occurs every time the food is eaten, especially if larger quantities are consumed.

A food intolerance is not the same as a food allergy or chemical sensitivity, where a small amount of food or chemicals added to food affect the body's immune system. And it is not the same as food poisoning, which is caused by the toxic substances that harmful microorganisms release when they spoil food. Instead, a food intolerance occurs when the body does not produce enough of the chemical or enzyme that the body needs to digest the food.

Life without lactase

One of the most common types of food intolerances is to cow's milk. This condition is called lactose intolerance. It occurs in people who lack an enzyme called lactase, which is released by the cells that line the small intestine wall. Lactase is needed to digest lactose, which is a sugar in milk. The symptoms of lactose intolerance include a bloated stomach and stomach cramps, trapped gas, nausea, and diarrhea.

Celiac disease

Some people have an allergic response to **gluten**—a protein found in cereal grains such as barley and wheat. This is known as celiac disease. When people with celiac disease eat foods that contain gluten, their immune system reacts by attacking cells that line the walls of the small intestine.

Signs and symptoms

The symptoms of celiac disease vary from person to person. Some people have no symptoms, but others may have diarrhea and stomach pains. Celiac disease causes other symptoms such as depression and irritability.

I suffer from celiac disease. It means I must check all foods carefully, as gluten can be found in everything from frozen yogurt to dried fruits to salad dressings.

Passing it on

Celiac disease is a genetic condition, which means parents pass it to their children. There is no cure for celiac disease. The best way to prevent the symptoms is to follow a strict gluten-free diet, avoiding foods that contain cereal grains.

Some people who suffer from celiac disease feel depressed and irritated much of the time.

FOOD FACTS AND STATS

A balanced diet needs to contain a proper mix of carbohydrates, fat, and protein. You can use the tables on these pages to help you choose different foods to ensure you get enough carbohydrates in your diet.

Examples of amount of actual carbohydrates in particular foods

Food	Carbohydrates
1 slice of white bread	0.4 oz (12 g)
1 medium-size banana	1 oz (27 g)
1 cup (240 ml) of spaghetti	1.2 oz (34 g)
1 large baked potato	2 oz (55 g)
3.6 oz (100 g) of cashew nuts	1oz (28 g)

Loading up on carbohydrates

Just one gram of carbohydrates provides four calories of energy. Athletes talk about carbohydrate loading and carbohydrate depletion. This refers to the amount of carbohydrate energy you can store in your muscles— about 2,000 carbohydrate calories. You can load up on carbohydrates or cut them out of your diet completely to change the amount of stored carbs in your body.

Recommended daily amounts of different kinds of food for children aged 9 to 13

Grains	5 oz (140 g) (girls) 6 oz (170 g) (boys)
Vegetables	2 cups (475 ml) (girls) 2.5 cups (600 ml) (boys)
Fruit	1.5 cups (350 ml)
Milk	3 cups (700 ml)
Meat and beans	5 oz (140 g)
Oils	5 teaspoons (25 ml)

Comparing calories

Energy in food is measured in calories. This is what 1 oz (28 g) gives:

Carbohydrate	105 calories
Protein	112 calories
Fat	252 calories

GLOSSARY

antibodies Proteins in the blood that destroy harmful germs in the body

antioxidant Mineral that mops up harmful products

arteries Blood vessels that carry blood away from the heart to the rest of the body

atom Smallest part of an element that can exist alone

calorie Unit measuring the amount of energy a food will produce

chyme Digestive juice

colon Lower part of the bowels, where food is changed into waste

diabetes Disease in which the body lacks insulin, resulting in high levels of sugar in the blood

enzyme Protein that helps to break down food in your system

esophagus Muscular tube that runs from your throat to your stomach

fatal Causing death

gluten Protein in some cereals

histamine Chemical substance produced during an allergic reaction

hormone Chemical released by cells or glands that controls processes in other parts of the body

immune system System that protects your body against disease

intestine Tube through which food passes after leaving the stomach

molecule Smallest part of a substance

nutrient Healthy source of nourishment

pectin Chemical substance found in some fruits that helps keep your heart healthy

peristalsis Waves of muscle contraction and relaxation that force food through the intestine

process To change or prepare food using several ingredients and other substances such as salt and chemicals

rectum Lowest part of your bowels

refined Made fine or pure by an industrial process

respiration Process of breathing

United States Department of Agriculture (USDA) Organization that deals with food production laws

FURTHER READING

Further Reading

Sayer, Dr. Melissa, *Too Fat? Too Thin? The Healthy Eating Guidebook*. Crabtree Publishing, 2009.

Doeden, Matt. *Eat Right*, Lerner, 2009.

Gardner, Robert. *Health Science Projects about Nutrition*. Enslow Publishers, 2002.

King, Hazel. *Carbohydrates for a Healthy Body*. Heinemann Library, 2009.

Internet

Harvard School of Public Health
www.hsph.harvard.edu/nutritionsource/
  what-should-you-eat/carbohydrates/

Your Digestive System
http://kidshealth.org/kid/htbw/
  digestive_system.html

Your Gross and Cool Body
http://yucky.discovery.com/flash/
  body/pg000126.html

Try this...

Keep a food journal. Write down everything you eat for an entire week. How much carbohydrate did you eat? Do you think you are eating enough carbs?

INDEX